MW01026960

# ENGINEERING REASONING

Based on Critical Thinking Concepts & Tools

SECOND EDITION

RICHARD PAUL, ROBERT NIEWOEHNER and LINDA ELDER

ROWMAN & LITTLEFIELD
Lanham • Boulder • New York • London

Originally published by
The Foundation for Critical Thinking
P. O. Box 196
Tomales, California 94971
www.criticalthinking.org

Reissued in 2019 by Rowman & Littlefield
An imprint of The Rowman & Littlefield Publishing Group, Inc.
4501 Forbes Boulevard, Suite 200, Lanham, Maryland 20706
www.rowman.com

6 Tinworth Street, London SE11 5AL, United Kingdom

British Library Cataloguing in Publication Information Available

**Library of Congress Cataloging-in-Publication Data**
Paul, Richard; Niewoehner, Robert; and Elder, Linda
The Thinker's Guide to Engineering Reasoning, Second Edition
Richard Paul
ISBN 978-0-944583-33-4 (pbk: alk. paper) | ISBN 978-1-5381-3379-8 (electronic)
1. Engineering 2. Engineering reasoning 3. Engineering education 4. Engineering instruction
5. Critical thinking 6. Rob Niewoehner 7. Linda Elder
2013949913

∞™ The paper used in this publication meets the minimum requirements of American National Standard for Information Sciences—Permanence of Paper for Printed Library Materials, ANSI/NISO Z39.48-1992.

# The Foundation for Critical Thinking and the Thinker's Guide Library

Founded by Dr. Richard Paul, the Foundation for Critical Thinking is the longest-running non-profit organization dedicated to critical thinking. Through seminars and conferences, online courses and resources, and a wide range of publications, the Foundation promotes critical societies by cultivating essential intellectual abilities and virtues in every field of study and professional area. Learn more at www.criticalthinking.org and visit the Center for Critical Thinking Community Online (criticalthinkingcommunity.org).

The Thinker's Guide Library introduces the Paul-Elder Framework for Critical Thinking™ and contextualizes critical thinking across subject areas and audience levels to foster fairminded critical reasoning throughout the world.

1. The Miniature Guide to Critical Thinking Concepts & Tools, Eighth Edition
2. The Thinker's Guide to Analytic Thinking
3. The Thinker's Guide to Ethical Reasoning
4. The Thinker's Guide to Socratic Questioning
5. The Thinker's Guide to Fallacies
6. The Nature and Functions of Critical & Creative Thinking
7. The Art of Asking Essential Questions, Fifth Edition
8. The Thinker's Guide to the Human Mind
9. The Thinker's Guide for Conscientious Citizens on How to Detect Media Bias and Propaganda in National and World News, Fourth Edition
10. The Thinker's Guide to Scientific Thinking
11. The Thinker's Guide to Engineering Reasoning
12. The Thinker's Guide to Clinical Reasoning
13. The Aspiring Thinker's Guide to Critical Thinking
14. The Student Guide to Historical Thinking
15. The Thinker's Guide for Students on How to Study & Learn a Discipline, Second Edition
16. How to Read a Paragraph: The Art of Close Reading, Second Edition
17. How to Write a Paragraph: The Art of Substantive Writing
18. The International Critical Thinking Reading and Writing Test, Second Edition
19. The Miniature Guide to Practical Ways for Promoting Active and Cooperative Learning, Third Edition
20. How to Improve Student Learning: 30 Practical Ideas
21. A Critical Thinker's Guide to Educational Fads
22. The Thinker's Guide to Intellectual Standards
23. A Guide for Educators to Critical Thinking Competency Standards

# Contents

# Foreword

I am delighted to recommend *The Thinker's Guide to Engineering Reasoning* for engineering instructors, students, and engineers alike. This guide is a very useful addition to the arsenal of engineering education tools. I believe it fills a gap that has been largely ignored in engineering instruction. It covers an important area of competence that we so often presume students will acquire, but traditionally (and sadly) do not sufficiently address, if at all.

An isolated focus on technical skill delivery, or on one skill area, has not worked in the past, currently fails and will not meet tomorrow's needs. It is important for the field of engineering to be understood as systems of overlapping and interrelated ideas, rather than isolated and different fields of knowledge. Moreover, it is important to recognize and effectively deal with the multiple environmental, social and ethical aspects that complicate responsible engineering. Accordingly, it is time for engineering educators to realize that effective engineering instruction cannot be based in memorization or technical calculation alone. Rather, it is essential that engineering students develop the generalizable critical thinking skills and dispositions necessary for effectively and professionally reasoning through the complex engineering issues and questions they will face as engineers. The authors outline and detail these skills and dispositions quite effectively in this guide.

I am further delighted to note the level of detailed sub distinctions covered in the guide. I believe it is Dave Merrill who originally claimed that expertise is defined by the number of detailed sub-divisions clearly made and qualified. As such, the authors have proven mastery!

Growing industry dissatisfaction with deficient engineering education has led to the inception of the CDIO™ Initiative. This international design addresses engineering education reform in its broader context. Active student participation forms an integral part of this solution. While not the exclusive aim or application of this guide, its potential to compliment such institutional reforms by equipping the student to step up to the challenges of independent reasoning, is particularly beneficial.

*The Thinkers Guide to Engineering Reasoning* is not only a must-read publication for engineering educators, but a vital guide and career long companion for students and engineers alike.

Dr. AB Steyn
University of Pretoria
South Africa
May 2006

# Introduction

## Why A Thinker's Guide to Engineering Reasoning?

This thinker's guide is designed for administrators, faculty, and students. It contains the essence of engineering reasoning concepts and tools. For faculty it provides a shared concept and vocabulary. For students it is a thinking supplement to any textbook for any engineering course. Faculty can use it to design engineering instruction, assignments, and tests. Students can use it to improve their perspective in any domain of their engineering studies.

General critical thinking skills apply to all engineering disciplines. For example, engineering reasoners attempt to be clear as to the purpose at hand and the question at issue. They question information, conclusions, and points of view. They strive to be accurate, precise, and relevant. They seek to think beneath the surface, to be logical, and objective. They apply these skills to their reading and writing as well as to their speaking and listening. They apply them in professional and personal life.

When this guide is used as a supplement to the engineering textbook in multiple courses, students begin to perceive applications of engineering reasoning to many domains in their lives. In addition, if their instructors provide examples of the application of engineering thinking to life, students begin to see good thinking as a tool for improving the quality of their lives.

If you are a student using this guide, get in the habit of carrying it with you to every engineering class. Consult it frequently in analyzing and synthesizing what you are learning. Aim for deep internalization of the principles you find in it—until using them becomes second nature.

While this guide has much in common with *A Thinker's Guide to Scientific Thinking*, and engineers have much in common with scientists, engineers and scientists pursue different fundamental purposes and are engaged in distinctively different modes of inquiry. This should become apparent as you read this guide.

# A Framework for Engineering Reasoning

The analysis and evaluation of our thinking as engineers requires a vocabulary of thinking and reasoning. The intellect requires a voice. The model on the facing page is not unique to engineering; indeed, its real power is its flexibility in adapting to any domain of life and thought. Other Thinkers' Guides in the Thinker's Guides library[1] apply this framework to other disciplines. Engineers and scientists are quite comfortable working within the context of conceptual models. We employ thermodynamic models, electrical models, mathematical models, computer models or even physical models fashioned from wood or clay. In this guide we apply a model or framework for thinking, an architecture whose purpose aids the analysis and evaluation of thought, through which we might improve our thought. A glance at other Thinkers' Guides reveals that only shifts of emphasis are required to apply this model to the sciences, the humanities, or the arts.

The framework depicted on the following page provides an overview of the entire guide, working from the base of the diagram up. The goal or endpoint is the development of the mature engineering thinker; therefore, that endpoint is described first with a brief discussion of the intellectual virtues as might be expressed in the practice of engineering.

Subsequently, the eight elements of thought are introduced. These are tools for the analysis of thinking in ones' own and others' thought. These elements are then exemplified and applied to analyzing texts, articles, reports, and entire engineering disciplines.

Next, the intellectual standards are introduced and exemplified. These constitute the thinker's *evaluation* tools. They are then woven together with the elements in several formats to demonstrate application of these *evaluation* standards to the *analysis* of our thinking.

Finally, the guide includes several case studies of excellent thinking and deficient thinking in engineering. It then concludes by treating a number of distinctive topics that touch on the engineering profession, such as aesthetics, ethics, and engineers' relationships with other professionals.

## Using this Thinker's Guide

As with the other guides in the *Thinker's Guide* series, the content in this guide is not to be read as straight prose; it is predominantly composed of numerous examples, mostly probing questions, of a substantive critical thinking model applied to the engineering context. These examples may be used in class exercises, as reference material, or as templates for out-of-class work, which students adapt to their own courses, disciplines, and projects. A broader discussion of the approach to critical thinking used in this guide can be found in resources and articles on the website of the Foundation for Critical Thinking, www.criticalthinking.org. For deeper understanding of the basic theory of critical thinking, we especially recommend the book, *Critical Thinking: Tools for Taking Charge of Your Professional and Personal Life,* also available from the Foundation for Critical Thinking.

[1]  See The Thinker's Guides Library on pp. 52-54.

**Engineers concerned with good thinking routinely apply *intellectual standards* to the *elements of thought* as they seek to develop the traits of a mature engineering mind.**

## THE STANDARDS

| | |
|---|---|
| Clarity | Precision |
| Accuracy | Significance |
| Relevance | Completeness |
| Logicalness | Fairness |
| Breadth | Depth |

Must be applied to

## THE ELEMENTS

| | |
|---|---|
| Purposes | Inferences |
| Questions | Concepts |
| Points of view | Implications |
| Information | Assumptions |

As we learn to develop

## INTELLECTUAL TRAITS

| | |
|---|---|
| Intellectual Humility | Intellectual Perseverance |
| Intellectual Autonomy | Confidence in Reason |
| Intellectual Integrity | Intellectual Empathy |
| Intellectual Courage | Fairmindedness |

# Intellectual Traits Essential to Engineering Reasoning

No engineer can claim perfect objectivity; engineers' work is unavoidably influenced by many variables, including their education, experiences, attitudes, beliefs, and level of intellectual arrogance.

Highly skilled engineers recognize the importance of cultivating intellectual dispositions. These attributes are essential to excellence of thought. They determine with what insight and integrity one thinks.

**Intellectual humility** is knowledge of ignorance, sensitivity to what you know and what you do not know. It implies being aware of your biases, prejudices, self-deceptive tendencies, and the limitations of your viewpoint and experience. Licensure as a Professional Engineer (PE) explicitly demands that engineers self-consciously restrict their professional judgments to those domains in which they are truly qualified.[2] Questions that foster intellectual humility in engineering thinking include:

- What do I really know about the technological issue I am facing?
- To what extent do my prejudices, attitudes, or experiences bias my judgment? Does my experience really qualify me to handle this issue?
- Am I quick to admit when I am dealing with a domain beyond my expertise?
- Am I open to considering novel approaches to this problem, and willing to learn and study where warranted?

**Intellectual courage** is the disposition to question beliefs about which you feel strongly. It includes questioning the beliefs of your culture and any subculture to which you belong, and a willingness to express your views even when they are unpopular (with management, peers, subordinates, or customers). Questions that foster intellectual courage include:

- To what extent have I analyzed the beliefs I hold which may impede my ability to think critically?
- To what extent have I demonstrated a willingness to yield my positions when sufficient evidence is presented against them?
- To what extent am I willing to stand my ground against the majority (even though people ridicule me)?

**Intellectual empathy** is awareness of the need to actively entertain views that differ from your own, especially those with which you strongly disagree. It entails accurately reconstructing the viewpoints and reasoning of your opponents and reasoning from premises, assumptions, and ideas other than your own. Questions that foster intellectual empathy include:

- To what extent do I listen and seek to understand others' reasoning?
- To what extent do I accurately represent viewpoints with which I disagree?
- To what extent do I accurately represent opponents' views? Would they agree?

2 National Society of Professional Engineers. 2003. *Code of Ethics for Engineers*. www.nspe.org/ethics/codeofethics2003.pdf.

- To what extent do I recognize and appreciate insights in the technical views of others and recognize prejudices in my own?

**Intellectual integrity** consists in holding yourself to the same intellectual standards you expect others to honor (no double standards). Questions that foster intellectual integrity in engineering reasoning include:

- To what extent do I expect of myself what I expect of others?
- To what extent are there contradictions or inconsistencies in the way I deal with technical issues?
- To what extent do I strive to recognize and eliminate self-deception and bad faith in my thinking when reasoning through engineering issues?

**Intellectual perseverance** is the disposition to work your way through intellectual complexities despite frustrations inherent in the task. Questions that foster intellectual perseverance in engineering reasoning include:

- Am I willing to work my way through complexities in an engineering issue or do I tend to give up when challenged?
- Can I think of a difficult engineering problem in which I have demonstrated patience and tenacity?
- Do I have strategies for dealing with complex engineering issues?

**Confidence in reason** is based on the belief that one's own higher interests and those of humankind at large are best served by giving the freest play to reason. It means using standards of reasonability as the fundamental criteria by which to judge whether to accept or reject any proposition or position. Questions that foster confidence in reason include:

- Am I willing to change my position when the evidence leads to a more reasonable position?
- Do I aalways try to follow the evidence, without regard to my own interests?
- Do I encourage others to come to their own conclusions or do I try to coerce agreement?

**Intellectual autonomy** is thinking for oneself while adhering to standards of rationality. It means thinking through issues using one's own thinking rather than uncritically accepting the viewpoints, opinions, and judgments of others. Questions that foster intellectual autonomy in engineering thinking include:

- To what extent do I uncritically accept what I am told (by my supervisors, peers, government, and so on)?
- To what extent do I uncritically accept traditional solutions to problems?
- Do I think through technical issues on my own or do I merely accept the conclusions or judgments of others?
- Having thought through an issue from a rational perspective, am I willing to stand alone against irrational criticism?

**Fairmindedness** is being conscious of the need to treat all viewpoints alike, without reference to one's own feelings or vested interests, or the feelings or vested interests of one's friends, company, community or nation. It implies adherence to intellectual standards without reference to one's own advantage or the advantage of one's group. Questions that foster fairmindedness include:

- To what extent do self-interests or biases tend to cloud my judgment?
- How do I tend to treat relevant viewpoints? Do I tend to favor some over others? And if so, why?
- To what extent do I appropriately weigh the strengths and weaknesses of all significant relevant perspectives when reasoning through an issue?
- What personal interests do we have at stake here and how can we ensure that we don't favor our own interests over the common good?

**Intellectual Curiosity** entails inquisitiveness as well as a strong desire to deeply understand, to figure things out, to propose and assess useful and plausible hypotheses and explanations; it implies a strong propensity to learn and to search out solutions; it propels the thinker toward further and deeper learning. Intellectually curious thinkers welcome and pursue complex, intriguing, and vexing questions. They reject superficial learning, or simplistic explanations. Intellectual perseverance is typically fueled by curiosity. The Columbia accident investigation board explicitly cited "intellectual curiosity" several times as the vital missing trait from NASA, contributing to the accident. Questions that foster intellectual curiosity in engineering reasoning include:

- To what extent do I search out new and powerful ways of addressing issues in engineering?
- To what extent do I go beyond surface explanations when dealing with complex issues?
- To what extent does my curiosity lead me to deeper insights and more powerful conceptualizations?
- To what extent do I accept traditional methods of reasoning through engineering issues, rather than seeking potentially more insightful methods?

**Essential Intellectual Virtues**

Intellectual Integrity

Intellectual Autonomy

Intellectual Humility

Intellectual Empathy

*Intellectual Traits or Virtues*

Confidence in Reason

Intellectual Courage

Intellectual Perseverance

Fairmindedness

# To Analyze Thinking We Must Learn to Identify and Question its Elemental Structures

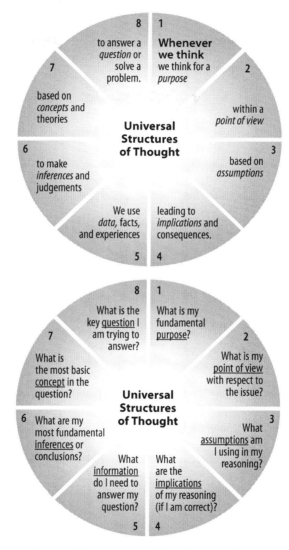

*Note:* When we understand the structures of thought, we ask important questions implied by these structures.

# A Checklist for Engineering Reasoning

1. **All engineering reasoning expresses a** *purpose.*
   - Have I distinguished my purpose from related purposes?
   - Have I checked periodically to be sure I am still on target?
   - Have I chosen realistic and achievable purposes?

2. **All engineering reasoning seeks to figure something out, to settle some** *question,* **solve some engineering** *problem.*
   - Have I stated the question at issue clearly and precisely?
   - Have I expressed the question in several ways to clarify its meaning and scope?
   - Have I divided the question into sub-questions?
   - Have I determined if the question has one right answer, or requires reasoning from more than one hypothesis or point of view?

3. **All engineering reasoning requires** *assumptions.*
   - Have I clearly identified my assumptions and determined whether they are justifiable?
   - Have I considered how my assumptions are shaping my point of view?
   - Have I considered which of my assumptions might be resonably questioned?

4. **All engineering reasoning is done from some perspective or** *point of view.*
   - Have I identified my specific point of view?
   - Have I considered the point of view of other stakeholders?
   - Have I striven to be fairminded in evaluating all relevant points of view?

5. **All engineering reasoning is based on** *data, information,* **and** *evidence.*
   - Have I validated my data sources?
   - Have I restricted my claims to those supported by the data?
   - Have I searched for data that opposes my position as well as alternative theories?
   - Have I ensured that all data used is clear, accurate, and relevant to the question at issue?
   - Have I ensured that I have gathered sufficient data?

6. **All engineering reasoning is expressed through, and shaped by,** *concepts* **and** *theories.*
   - Have I identified key concepts and explained them clearly?
   - Have I considered alternative concepts or alternative definitions of concepts?
   - Have I distorted ideas to fit my agenda?

7. **All engineering reasoning entails** *inferences* **or** *interpretations* **by which we draw** *conclusions* **and give meaning to engineering data and work.**
   - Have I inferred only what the data supports?
   - Have I checked inferences for their internal and external consistency?
   - Have I identified assumptions that led to my conclusions?

8. **All engineering reasoning leads somewhere or has** *implications* **and** *consequences.*
   - Have I traced the implications that follow from the data and from my reasoning?
   - Have I searched for negative as well as positive implications (technical, social, environmental, financial, ethical)?
   - Have I considered all significant implications?

# The Spirit of Critical Thinking

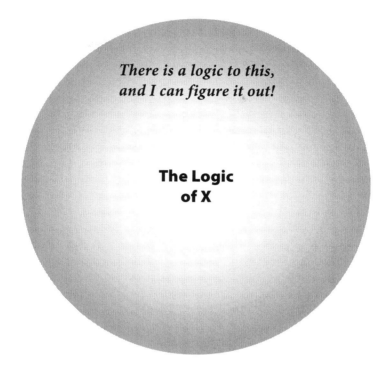

*There is a logic to this, and I can figure it out!*

**The Logic of X**

**Be aware:** Highly skilled engineers have confidence in their ability to figure out the logic of anything they choose. They continually look for order, system and interrelationships.

# Analyzing an Engineering Document

One important way to understand an engineering article, text or technical report, is through analysis of the structure of an author's reasoning. Once you have done this, you can then evaluate the author's reasoning using intellectual standards (see page 26). Here is a template to use:

1.  The main *purpose* of this engineering article is _____.

    *(State, as accurately as possible, the author's purpose for writing the document. What was the author trying to accomplish?)*

2.  The key *question* that the author is addressing is _____.

    *(Your goal is to figure out the key question that was in the mind of the author when s/he wrote the article. In other words, what key question is addressed?)*

3.  The most important *information* in this engineering article is

    _____.

    *(Identify the key information the author used, or presupposed, in the article to support his/her main arguments. Here you are looking for facts, experiences, and/or data the author is using to support her/his conclusions, as well as its sources.)*

4.  The main *inferences*/conclusions in this article are

    _____.

    *(Identify the most important conclusions that the author reaches and presents in the article.)*

5.  The key *concepts* we need to understand in this engineering article are

    _____.

    By these *ideas* the author means _____.

    *(To identify these concepts, ask yourself, What are the most important ideas or theories you would have to understand in order to understand the author's line of reasoning? Then briefly elaborate what the author means by these ideas.)*

# Analyzing an Engineering Document (cont'd)

6.  The main *assumption*(s) underlying the author's thinking is (are)
    _____.

    *(Ask yourself, What is the author taking for granted [that might be questioned]? The assumptions are generalizations that the author does not think require defense in this context, and they are usually unstated. This is where the author's thinking logically begins.)*

7a. If we take this line of reasoning seriously, the *implications* are
    _____.

    *(What consequences are likely to follow if people accept the author's line of reasoning? Here you are to follow out the logical implications of the author's position. You should include implications the author states, but also include those the author does not state.)*

7b. If we fail to take this line of reasoning seriously, the *implications* are
    _____.

    *(What consequences are likely to follow if people ignore the author's reasoning?)*

8.  The main *point(s) of view* presented in this engineering article is (are)
    _____.

    *(The main question you are trying to answer here is, What is the author looking at, and how is s/he seeing it? For example, in this guide we are looking at engineering reasoning and seeing it "as requiring intellectual discipline and the development of intellectual skills.")*

If you understand these structures as they interrelate in an engineering article, or technical report, you should be able to empathically role-play the thinking of the author. Remember, the eight basic structures of thought highlighted here define all reasoning, regardless of discipline or domain of thought. By extension, they are also the essential elements of engineering reasoning.

# Analyzing a Design Using the Elements of Thought

**Engineering purpose**
What is the purpose of this design?
What are the market opportunities or mission requirements?
Who defines market opportunities/mission requirements?
Who is the customer?

**Question at hand**
What system/product/process will best satisfy the customer's performance, cost, and schedule requirements?
How does the customer define "value"?
Is a new design or new technology required?
Can an existing design be adapted?
How important is time-to-market?

**Point of view**
A design and manufacturing point of view is typically presumed. What other points of view deserve consideration? Stockholders? Component vendors/suppliers? Marketing/sales? Customers? Maintenance/repair/parts? Regulators? Community affairs? Politicians? Environmentalists?

**Assumptions**
What environmental or operating conditions are assumed?
What programmatic, financial, market or technical risks have been considered acceptable to date?
What market/economic/competitive environment is assumed?
What safety/environmental assumptions are we making? Are these assumptions acceptable?
What maturity level or maturation timeline is assumed for emerging technologies?
What happens if we change or discard an assumption?
What criteria have historically been assumed in defining a "best" or "optimum" solution?
What assumptions have been made on the availability of materials?
What manufacturing capability was assumed?
What workforce skills or attributes have been assumed?

# Analyzing a Design Using the Elements of Thought (cont'd)

**Engineering information**
What is the source of supporting information (handbook, archival literature, experimentation, corporate knowledge, building codes, government regulation)?

What information do we lack? How can we get it? Analysis? Simulation? Component testing? Prototypes?

What experiments should be conducted?

Have we considered all relevant sources?

What legacy solutions, shortcomings, or problems should be studied and evaluated?

Is the available information sufficient? Do we need more data? What is the best way to collect it?

Have analytical or experimental results been confirmed?

What insights and experiences can the shop floor provide?

**Concepts**
What concepts or theories are applicable to this problem?

Are there competing models?

What emerging theory might provide insight?

What available technologies or theories are appropriate?

What emerging technologies might soon be applicable?

**Inferences**
What is the set of viable candidate solutions?

Why were other candidate solutions rejected?

Is there another way to interpret the information?

Is the conclusion practicable and affordable?

**Implications**
What are some important implications of the data we have gathered?

What are the most important market implications of the technology?

What are the most important implications of a key technology not maturing on time?

How important is after-market sustainability?

Is there a path for future design evolution and upgrade?

Are there disposal/end-of-service-life issues we need to consider?

What are the most important implications of product failure?

What design features if changed, profoundly affect other design features?

What design features are insensitive to other changes?

What potential benefits do by-products offer?

Should social reaction and change management issues be addressed?

# Two Kinds of Engineering Questions

In approaching a question, it is helpful to determine the kind of system to which it belongs. Is it a question with one definitive answer? Alternatively, does the question require us to consider competing answers or even competing approaches to either solution or conceptualization?

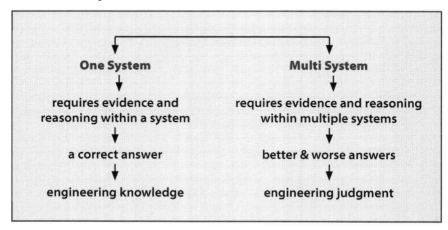

**Questions of Procedure** (established system)—Questions with an established procedure or method for finding the answer. These questions are settled by facts, by definition, or both. They are prominent in mathematics as well as the physical and biological sciences. Examples include:
- What materials do building codes require for this application?
- What is the yield strength of this material?
- How much electrical power does this equipment need?
- How hot does this fuel burn?

**Questions of Judgment** (conflicting systems)—Questions requiring reasoned judgment, and with more than one arguable answer. These are questions that make sense to debate, questions with better-or-worse answers (well-supported and reasoned or poorly-supported and/or poorly-reasoned answers). Here we are seeking the best answer within a range of possibilities. We evaluate answers to such questions using universal intellectual standards such as breadth, depth, logicalness, and fairness. Some of the most important engineering questions are conflicting-system questions (for example, those questions with an ethical dimension). Examples include:
- How long will this part last?
- Should the development follow a spiral or waterfall management model?
- Is the customer most concerned with cost or performance?
- How does the customer define "acceptable risk?"
- What model should be employed to reduce environment impact?

# Analyzing Disciplines: Aerospace Engineering

**Purpose.** Aerospace Engineering develops aerial and space-based systems for defense, scientific, commercial, civil, and recreational markets and missions. General mission needs within those markets include transportation, earth and space sensing, and communications. Typically, the products are vehicles such as rockets, airplanes, missiles, satellites, and spacecraft, although the product may also include the ground support equipment, or imbedded hardware or software.

**Key Question(s).** What are the detailed design features of the system that best satisfy the stated mission or market requirement? How will we design, build, test, fabricate, and support aerospace vehicles?

**Point of View.** The conceptual mission profile typically provides the organizing framework for all design requirements and design decisions. The attempt is to define value principally from the perspective of the organizational leader who is sending the vehicle on some mission flight (and paying for the flight). Other perspectives may also be relevant: pilots, maintainers, manufacturing, and logisticians, as well as technologists (structural engineers, aerodynamicists, controls engineers, propulsion engineers, and relevant others). Politicians will likely be influential in large aerospace programs. Public opinion, concerned with ethical or environmental issues, are often relevant, and if so, must be considered.

**Key Concepts.** These include all those concepts associated with classical physics, with some particular emphases: Newtonian and orbital mechanics, conservation of mass, momentum and energy, low and high speed aerodynamics, material properties and lightweight structures, propulsion technologies.

**Key Assumptions.** Assumptions are in part shared by all scientists and engineers. One assumption is that the universe is controlled by pervasive laws that can be expressed in mathematical terms and formulas. Additionally, aerospace engineers assume that an aerospace solution will invariably entail the integration of multiple technological disciplines and the resolution of competing design tensions, including aerodynamics, astrodynamics, stability and control, propulsion, structures, and avionics. Furthermore, the aerospace system will be a system of systems, which must also fit and interface with a larger system (e.g., air cargo airplanes must fit and communicate with the air traffic control structures, missiles must fit with existing launch rails; satellites must fit on independently developed launch vehicles).

**The Data or Information.** Aerospace engineers employ experimental and computational data, legacy designs, regulatory requirements, market studies or mission needs statements.

**Inferences, Generalizations, or Hypotheses.** The conclusion of most aerospace engineering activity is a product ready for delivery to a customer.

**Implications.** Aerospace engineering products and services have wide-ranging implications, linked with global, national, local economics, ethics, defense, security, environmental effects such as noise and pollution, and infrastructure such as airports, any of which may impact the quality of life in communities and regions.

# Analyzing Disciplines: Electrical Engineering

**Purpose.** Electrical engineering develops electrical and electronic systems for public, commercial, and consumer markets. It is tremendously broad, spanning many domains including recreational electronics, residential lighting, space communications, and electrical utilities.

**Key Questions.** What are the detailed design features of the system that best satisfy the stated mission or market requirements? How will we conceive, design, implement, and operate electrical and electronic products and systems?

**Point of View.** The point of view is commonly that of the design and manufacturing team. Other relevant points of view include the customer, stockholders, marketing, maintainers, or operators.

**Key Concepts.** These concepts include electromagnetism (Maxwell's equations), electrochemical properties of materials, discrete and analog mathematics, resistance, current, charge, voltage, fields and waves, and so on.

**Key Assumptions.** Assumptions are in part shared by all scientists and engineers. One assumption is that the universe is controlled by pervasive laws that can be expressed in mathematical terms and formulas, and that those principles can be used to model electrical systems. Electrical engineers assume that some important market needs can be best met through electrical and electronic products. Additionally, electrical engineers frequently assume that their work must be integrated with other engineering disciplines (such as mechanical, chemical, and so forth) in the design and implementation of a product.

**Data or Information.** Electrical engineers employ experimental and computational data, legacy designs, regulatory requirements, market studies or mission needs statements.

**Inferences, Generalizations, or Hypotheses.** The conclusion of most electrical engineering activity is a product ready for delivery to a customer.

**Implications.** Electrical engineering products and services have wide-ranging implications that span global, national, and local economics, public infrastructure, health care, and communications, with potential for positive and negative quality of life impacts on communities and regions.

# Analyzing Disciplines: Mechanical Engineering

**Purpose.** Mechanical engineering develops mechanical systems and materials for public, commercial, and consumer markets. It is tremendously broad, spanning transportation, mechanisms, architecture, energy systems, materials, and more.

**Key Questions.** What are the detailed design features of the mechanical system that best satisfy the stated mission or market requirement? How will we conceive, design, implement, and operate mechanical components, products, and systems?

**Point of View.** Commonly, the point of view is that of the design and manufacturing team. Other relevant points of view include the customer, stockholders, marketing, maintainers, or operators.

**Key Concepts.** These concepts include materials science, stress, strain, loads, friction, dynamics, statics, thermodynamics, fluid mechanics, energy, work, CAD/CAM, machines, and so on.

**Key Assumptions.** Assumptions are in part shared by all scientists and engineers. One assumption is that the universe is controlled by pervasive laws that can be expressed in mathematical terms and formulas, and that those principles can be used to model mechanical systems. Mechanical engineers assume that market needs can be met with mechanisms and materials. Additionally, mechanical engineers frequently must integrate their work with other engineering disciplines (such as automotive, aerospace, electrical, computer, chemical, and so forth) in the design and implementation of a product.

**Data or Information.** Mechanical engineers require experimental and computational data, legacy designs, regulatory requirements, market studies or mission need statements.

**Inferences, Generalizations, or Hypotheses.** The conclusion of most mechanical engineering activity is a product ready for delivery to a customer, or integration into a larger system.

**Implications.** Mechanical engineering products and services have wide-ranging implications that span global, national, and local economics, public infrastructure, transportation, health care and communications with potential for positive and negative quality of life impacts on communities and regions.

*Braine-le-Château (Belgium), the old community watermill on the Hain river. Picture by Jean-Pol GRANDMONT*

# Analyzing Engineering Tools:
# Modeling and Simulation

**Purpose.** Modeling and simulation can either be a direct engineering product or a development tool used to design other complex systems. It provides a representation of the physical world for purposes such as operator training, development trade studies, component development, prototype testing, and test and evaluation where full-scale live testing is impractical, dangerous or cost-prohibitive.

**Key Questions.** How can the features of the real world be practically simulated to provide accurate insight into physical interactions and behaviors in order to design physical systems for specific purposes? What level of detail is required for accurate portrayal of the systems behavior?

**Point of View.** Simulation and modeling takes the point of view that the physical world submits to mathematical and computational modeling to such an extent that the behaviors observed in simulation reliably imitate or predict a system's performance in the real world.

**Key Concepts.** Concepts span all domains of engineering, but also notably include concepts such as numerical methods, equations of motion, man-the-loop and hardware-in-the-loop testing, batch simulation, virtual reality, display latency, systems identification and computational throughput.

**Key Assumptions.** Simulation depends upon simplifying assumptions; real world detail remains beyond our reach. Simple simulations entail lengthy lists of assumptions. Improving simulation fidelity entails adding details to physical models that are assumed negligible in more simple models. Enhancing fidelity to the real physical world means removing assumptions, and consequently building complexity.

- When using modeling and simulation, engineers assume that they can design models that accurately represent the physical world to a sufficient level of detail.
- Simulation and modeling typically assumes that a relationship exists between cost and complexity, value and fidelity.
- Engineers assume that there are situations in which modeling and simulation provides vital insight (note that simulation may be employed throughout the product life, from conception to operation), while simultaneously recognizing that unmodeled phenomena may indeed be significant (limiting the simulations value).

**The Data or Information.** The information upon which simulation and modeling depends includes math models for the interaction of simulated systems, plus specific attributes of physical systems provided by analysis, physical testing, legacy designs, or systems identification.

**Inferences.** Simulation conclusions include design decisions as well as training and educational practices.

**Implications.** Simulation can reduce the risk or expense of engineering development and testing, or provide insight into a system's response to conditions which cannot practically or safely be tested in realistic conditions (e.g., failure states or emergency conditions). However, if a simulation product or process is flawed, negative implications might exist for the use of the actual product when used in the real world.

# Skilled Engineers Consentingly Adhere to Intellectual Standards

Universal intellectual standards must be applied to thinking whenever one is evaluating the quality of reasoning as one reasons through problems, issues, and questions. These standards are not unique to engineering, but are universal to all domains of thinking. To think as a highly skilled engineer entails having command of these standards and regularly applying them to thought. While there are a number of universal standards, we focus here on some of the most significant.

**Clarity:** Understandable; the meaning can be grasped

*Clarity is a gateway standard. If a statement is unclear, we cannot determine whether it is accurate or relevant. In fact, we cannot tell anything about it because we do not yet know what it is saying.*

Questions targeting clarity include the following.

- Could you elaborate further on that point?
- Could you express that point in another way?
- Could you give me an illustration or example?
- Are the market/mission requirements clearly stated?
- Have terms and symbols been clearly defined?
- Which requirements have priority and which can be relaxed if required?
- Have the assumptions been clearly stated?
- Is specialized terminology either defined, or being used in keeping with educated usage?
- Do drawings/graphs/photos and supporting annotations clearly portray important relationships?[3]
- How do the affected stakeholders define "value"?

**Accuracy:** Free from errors or distortions; true

*A statement can be clear but not accurate, as in "Most creatures with a spine are over 300 pounds in weight."*

Questions targeting accuracy include the following.

- Is that really true?
- How could we check that?
- How could we find out if that is true?
- What is your confidence in that data?
- Has the test equipment been calibrated? How or when?

---

[3] See pp. 27-28 for further questions that target the assessment of graphics through intellectual standards. Students and faculty interested in clarity of graphical communication are urged to read these three books by Edward Tufte: *Visual Explanations, Envisioning Information,* and *The Visual Display of Quantitative Information.* Published by Graphics Press, Cheshire, Connecticut.

- How have simulation models been validated?
- Have assumptions been challenged for legitimacy?
- What if the environment is other than we had expected (e.g., hotter, colder, dusty, humid)?
- Are there hidden or unstated assumptions that should be challenged?

**Precision:** Exact to the necessary level of detail

> *A statement can be both clear and accurate, but not precise, as in "The solution in the beaker is hot." (We don't know how hot it is.)*

Engineering questions targeting precision include the following.

- Could you give me more details?
- Could you be more specific?
- What are acceptable tolerances for diverse pieces of information?
- What are the error bars or confidence bounds on experimental, handbook or analytical data?
- At what threshold do details or additional features no longer add value?

**Concision:** Brief in form while comprehensive in scope, implies the elimination of unnecessary details to clarify thought

> *Concision does not connote eliminating words for brevity's sake (the sound bite), but rather an economy of thoughts whereby the thinking is deep and significant, and clarity is actually enhanced by the limited use of words. The question – or questions – at issue, and the context within which the question is situated, determine the amount of detail needed to clarify or guide thought in a given situation. In other words the question, and its context, drive the level of detail (precision/concision) needed. In the hours building to the loss of the Space Shuttle Challenger, engineers understood the peril faced by launching at extremely low temperatures. Yet, they buried their management in insignificant details such that their message was missed; their signal was lost in self-generated noise. "Clear and concise" appear routinely in business writing guides as almost inseparable expectations of business leaders. In his Principia, Isaac Newton remarked, "More is vain when less will serve."*

Questions targeting concision include the following:

- What can I remove that will boost the clarity of my point?
- Do I need to eliminate any distracting details?
- Should I move some of the relevant data to an appendix where it is available but less distracting (because less important)?
- Can a graph more concisely present this tabulated data, and boost the clarity of the data being presented and the variables being considered?

**Relevance:** Relating to the matter at hand

> *A statement can be clear, accurate, and precise, but not relevant to the question at issue. A technical report might mention the time of day and phase of the moon*

*at which the test was conducted. This would be relevant if the system under test were a night vision device. It would be irrelevant if it were a microwave oven.*

Questions targeting relevance include the following.

- How is that connected to the question?
- How does that bear on the issue?
- Have all relevant factors been weighed (e.g., environmental, or marketplace)?
- Are there unnecessary details obscuring the dominant factors?
- Has irrelevant data been included?
- Have important interrelationships been identified and studied?
- Have features and capabilities (and hence costs) been included which the customer neither needs nor wants?

**Depth:** Containing complexities and multiple interrelationships

*A statement can be clear, accurate, precise, and relevant, but superficial. For example, the statement, "Radioactive waste from nuclear reactors threatens the environment," is clear, accurate, and relevant. Nevertheless, more details and further reasoning need to be added to transform the initial statement into the beginnings of a deep analysis.*

Questions targeting depth include the following.

- How does your analysis address the complexities in the question?
- How are you taking into account the problems in the question?
- Is that dealing with the most significant factors?
- Does this design model have adequate complexity and detail, given its counterpart in reality?

**Breadth:** Encompassing multiple viewpoints

*A line of reasoning may be clear, accurate, precise, relevant, and deep, but lack breadth (as in an argument from either of two conflicting theories, both consistent with available evidence).*

Questions targeting multiple viewpoints include the following.

- Do we need to consider another point of view?
- Is there another way to look at this question?
- What would this look like from the point of view of a conflicting theory, hypothesis, or conceptual scheme?
- Have the full range of options been explored?
- Have interactions with other systems been fully considered?

**Logic:** The parts make sense together, no contradictions

*When we think, we bring a variety of thoughts together into some order. The thinking is "logical" when the conclusion follows from the supporting data or*

Questions/Statements targeting logic include the following.
- Does this really make sense?
- Does that follow from what you said? How does that follow?
- But earlier you implied this and now you are saying that. I don't see how both can be true.
- Are the design decisions supported by logical analysis?

**Fairness:** Justifiable, not self-serving or one-sided

> *Fairness is particularly at play where more than one viewpoint is relevant to understanding and reasoning through an issue (conflicting conceptual systems), or where there are conflicting interests among stakeholders. Fairness gives all relevant perspectives a voice, while recognizing that not all perspectives may be equally valuable or important.*

Questions targeting fairness include the following.
- Have other points of view been considered (stock holders, manufacturing, sales, customers, maintenance, public citizens, community interests, and so on)?
- Are vested interests inappropriately influencing the design?
- Are divergent views within the design team given fair consideration?
- Have the environmental/safety impacts been appropriately weighed?
- Have we fully considered the public interest?
- Have we thought through the ethical implications in this decision?

**Significance:** Important, of consequence

> *Our thought can be clear, accurate, precise, and relevant, yet be trivial, or fail to focus on significant issues or problems. Engineering frequently entails problems with multiple relevant independent variables, and yet one or two out of a half dozen may outstrip the others in importance or significance. Students can grasp at anything that comes to mind that's relevant, and yet miss the significant. This is also common in poorly run meetings, in which minor matters consume inordinate time, and vital issues get short shrift or are ignored entirely. Attentiveness to the significant results in recognizing the most important information, issues and implications in engineering reasoning.*

Questions targeting significance include the following:
- Have we identified the most important questions at the heart of the issue?
- What are the most influential factors?
- What are the important variables that need to be considered?
- What are the most significant implications that must be reasoned through as we design this project?

# Universal Intellectual Standards Essential to Sound Engineering Reasoning

| Clarity | Could you elaborate further?<br>Could you give me an example?<br>Could you illustrate what you mean? |

| Accuracy | How could we check on that?<br>How could we find out if that is true?<br>How could we verify or test that? |

| Precision | Could you be more specific?<br>Could you give me more details?<br>Could you be more exact? |

| Relevance | How does that relate to the problem?<br>How does that bear on the question?<br>How does that help us with the issue? |

| Depth | What factors make this a difficult problem?<br>What are some of the complexities of this question?<br>What are some of the difficulties we need to deal with? |

| Breadth | Do we need to look at this from another perspective?<br>Do we need to consider another point of view?<br>Do we need to look at this in other ways? |

| Logic | Does all this make sense together?<br>Are we taking a reasonable approach to the problem?<br>Does what you say follow from the evidence? |

| Significance | Is this the most important problem to consider?<br>Is this the central idea to focus on?<br>Which of these facts are most important? |

| Fairness | Am I considering the views of others in good faith?<br>Am I accurately representing the viewpoints of others?<br>Is there an ethical component to this issue that we are avoiding for reasons of vested interest? |

# Using Intellectual Standards to Assess Design Features

**Clarity**        Have the requirements been clearly defined
                   (cost/schedule/performance/interoperability)?
                   Are test standards clearly defined?
                   What are the success criteria?

**Accuracy**       Are the modeling assumptions appropriate to their application?
                   How have analytical or experimental results been confirmed?

**Precision**      What degree of detail is required in the design or simulation models?
                   What is the confidence range for the supporting data?
                   What variability can be expected in a material or manufacturing process?

**Depth**          Have the complexities of the problem been adequately addressed?
                   Does the design provide appropriate interface with other current or
                   projected systems with which it must interoperate?
                   Has growth capability been considered/addressed?
                   Will additional staff training or education be required?
                   Does the design take advantage of the design space?
                   Has software/hardware obsolescence been considered over the system
                   lifecycle?
                   Have end-of-life issues been identified?

**Breadth**        Have alternative approaches been considered?
                   Are there alternative or emergent technologies which offer cost or
                   performance gains?

**Relevance**      Does the design address the requirements?
                   Is there unnecessary over-design?
                   Are there unnecessary features?

**Significance**   Are we dealing with the most significant design issues?
                   What factors significantly drive or constrain the design?

**Fairness**       Have customer/supplier interests been properly weighed?
                   Have public or community interests been considered?

# Using Intellectual Standards to Assess Graphics

Technical documents and presentations commonly rely upon photographs, illustrations, and graphs to communicate content. Graphics are prominent because: (1) graphics can be very information dense; (2) graphics can reveal comparisons and trends that would be obscure in tabular data or text; and (3) graphics can reveal interconnections and relationships that are difficult to capture within the linear flow of text. Graphics *can* do these things, but *don't necessarily* do these things. Graphical evidence can also trivialize, mislead, obscure, or confuse.

Professor Edward Tufte (Yale) emphasizes the following paragraph as the most important message in any of his books on graphical communications.

> Visual representations of evidence should be governed by principles of reasoning about quantitative evidence. For information displays, design reasoning must correspond to scientific reasoning. Clear and precise seeing becomes as one with clear and precise thinking.[4]

Thus, intellectual standards apply to graphical communication as well as they do to other forms of information!

## Clarity

- Will color enhance this graphic's clarity? (Frequently, "Yes")
- Must I plan for black and white reproduction? (Also frequently, "Yes")
- Have symbols been defined? Could annotation replace symbols?
- Are units of measure clearly labeled?
- Are consistent units and axes warranted?
- Must the graphic stand by itself? Alternatively, can it rely on nearby text?
- Could multiple graphs be overlaid to improve comparisons?
- Is data running together? Should these graphs be separate?

## Precision

- Will this graphic be presented on paper, or must I account for low-resolution media, which lose detail (e.g., web or computer projection)?
- Have I chosen appropriate axes? Should one axis be logarithmic?
- Would confidence bands or error bars improve credibility?

## Accuracy

- Is the choice of perspective or axes misleading?
- Are observed trends realistically portrayed or illegitimately amplified or attenuated by visual gimmick or distorted axes?

---

[4] Tufte E. 1997. *Visual Explanations*. Cheshire, Connecticut: Graphics Press, 53.

## Relevance

Automated software tools, clip art, and logos are notorious for adding visual fluff that dilutes content by raising the visual background noise (lowering signal-to-noise ratio). Relevant graphics serve the content by fostering understanding and retention.

- Does every dot of ink serve the content?
- Are grid lines really necessary? If so, are they as faint as possible?
- Does this graphic help the consumer better understand the content?
- Are all relevant factors displayed?

## Significance

- Does the graphic highlight significant concepts and relationships?
- Does a graphic artificially amplify insignificant relationships?
- Would another format better portray significant features?

## Breadth

- Are all relevant visual perspectives represented?

## Complexity/Depth

- Does my graphic suggest unrealistic simplicity?
- Is this graphic unnecessarily complicated?
- Does this graphic appropriately depict the complexities in the issue?
- Would a broader time scale provide a better context?
- Has truncated time history data artificially amplified random variation over a short time scale?

## Efficiency

Efficiency did not appear in our prior list of intellectual standards. It appears here because efficient use of paper or screen frequently requires the careful integration of graphical elements and data in ways that boost clarity and breadth, and enhance the revelation of complex interactions (e.g., causal relationships or contrasts). Graphical efficiency complements other intellectual standards. Tufte notes:

> Graphical excellence consists of complex ideas communicated with clarity, precision and efficiency. Graphical excellence is that which gives the viewer the greatest number of ideas in the shortest time with the least amount of ink.[5]

- Could multiple graphs be overlaid to fall within one page or screen?
- Can I get all the similar graphs onto a single page to improve the visibility of trends and to encourage direct comparison?
- Are the relevant visual perspectives accurately represented?
- Are the relevant visual perspectives properly weighted?

---

[5] Tufte E. 1997. *Visual Display of Quantitative Information*. Graphics Press, Cheshire, Connecticut, 51.

# Evaluating an Engineer's or Author's Reasoning

Evaluating reasoning entails applying intellectual standards to the elements of reasoning.

| Elements of Reasoning | Relevant Intellectual Standards |
|---|---|
| **Purpose** | |
| Is the report's (design's) purpose clearly stated or implied? | Clarity |
| Has information irrelevant to the purpose been included? | Relevance |
| | |
| **Questions** | |
| Is the specific question at issue focused? | Precision |
| Are the explicit questions relevant to the stated purpose? | Relevance |
| Does the question lay out the complexities in the issue? | Depth |
| Are the unanswered questions clearly identified? | Clarity |
| Does the question guide us to consider all relevant viewpoints? | Breadth |
| | |
| **Data or Information** | |
| What data is presented? | Clarity |
| What was measured? | Clarity |
| How was it measured and processed? | Accuracy |
| What were the limits of the instrumentation's precision? | Precision |
| Did the available precision capture the required detail? | Precision |
| What were the sources of data? Archival/Experimental/ Analytical/Modeling/Simulation? | Accuracy/ depth |
| Is the data accurate? How was accuracy established? | Accuracy |
| Is there data missing? Is there adequate data? | Accuracy |
| Is the data of sufficient quality? | Accuracy |
| What controls were applied to isolate causal factors? | Accuracy |
| Is the entire data set presented? What criteria were used to select the presented data sample from the complete data set? | Accuracy/ depth |
| | |
| **Key Concepts** | |
| Are key concepts identified? | Clarity |
| Are appropriate theories applied? | Relevance |
| Are the applicable theories suitably explained or referenced? | Depth |
| Have alternative concepts been considered? | Depth |
| Are concepts used justifiably? | Justifiability |

# Evaluating an Engineer's or Author's Reasoning, cont.

Evaluating reasoning entails applying intellectual standards to the elements of reasoning.

| Elements of Reasoning | Relevant Intellectual Standards |
|---|---|
| **Point of View** | |
| Is the author's point of view evident? | Clarity |
| Are there competing theories that could explain the data? | Breadth |
| Have alternative relevant viewpoints been fully considered? | Breadth |
| Have relevant viewpoints been ignored or distorted due to selfish or vested interests? | Fairness |
| Have alternative ways of looking at the situation been avoided in order to maintain a particular view? | Fairness |
| Have objections been addressed? | Fairness |
| | |
| **Assumptions** | |
| What is being assumed? | Clarity |
| Are the assumptions articulated/acknowledged? | Clarity |
| Are these assumptions legitimate or necessary? | Justifiability |
| Do the assumptions take into account the problem's complexity? | Depth |
| Are there alternative assumptions that should be considered? | Justifiability |
| | |
| **Inferences** | |
| Are the conclusions clearly stated? | Clarity |
| Does the data support the conclusion? | Logic |
| Are the conclusions important? | Significance |
| Are there alternative conclusions? | Logic |
| Is speculation misrepresented as fact? | Accuracy |
| Is complexity trivialized or acknowledged? | Depth |
| Do the conclusion follow from the assumptions? | Logic |
| | |
| **Implications** | |
| Are recommendations clearly presented? | Clarity |
| Is further testing required? | Depth |
| Why are these findings significant? | Significance |
| Do the conclusions have application beyond the question at hand? | Logic |
| Have other plausible implications been considered? | Logic |
| What implications follow if any assumptions prove unfounded? | Logic |

# Analyzing & Assessing Engineering Research

### Use this template to assess the quality of any engineering research project or paper.

1) All engineering research has a fundamental PURPOSE and goal.
   - Research purposes and goals should be clearly stated.
   - Related purposes should be explicitly distinguished.
   - All segments of the research should be relevant to the purpose.
   - All research purposes should be realistic and significant.

2) All engineering research addresses a fundamental QUESTION, problem or issue.
   - The fundamental question at issue should be clearly and precisely stated.
   - Related questions should be articulated and distinguished.
   - All segments of the research should be relevant to the central question.
   - All research questions should be realistic and significant.
   - All research questions should define clearly stated intellectual tasks that, being fulfilled, settle the questions.

3) All engineering research identifies data, INFORMATION, and evidence relevant to its fundamental question and purpose.
   - All information used should be clear, accurate, and relevant to the fundamental question at issue.
   - Information gathered must be sufficient to settle the question at issue.
   - Information contrary to the main conclusions of the research should be explained.

4) All engineering research contains INFERENCES or interpretations by which conclusions are drawn.
   - All conclusions should be clear, accurate, and relevant to the key question at issue.
   - Conclusions drawn should not go beyond what the data imply.
   - Conclusions should be consistent and reconcile discrepancies in the data.
   - Conclusions should explain how the key questions at issue have been settled.

5) All engineering research is conducted from some POINT OF VIEW or frame of reference.
   - All points of view in the research should be identified.
   - Objections from competing points of view should be identified and fairly addressed.

6) All engineering research is based on ASSUMPTIONS.
   - Clearly identify and assess major assumptions in the research.
   - Explain how the assumptions shape the research point of view.

7) All engineering research is expressed through, and shaped by, CONCEPTS and ideas.
   - Assess for clarity the key concepts in the research.
   - Assess the significance of the key concepts in the research.

8) All engineering research leads somewhere (i.e., have IMPLICATIONS and consequences).
   - Trace the implications and consequences that follow from the research.
   - Search for negative as well as positive implications.
   - Consider all significant implications and consequences.

# Purpose

(All reasoning has a purpose.)

**Primary Standards:** (1) Clarity, (2) Significance, (3) Achievability
(4) Consistency, (5) Justifiability

**Common Problems:** (1) Unclear, (2) Trivial, (3) Unrealistic, (4) Contradictory,
(5) Unfair

**Principle:** To reason well, you must clearly understand your purpose, and
your purpose must be reasonable and fair.

| Skilled Thinkers... | Unskilled Thinkers... | Critical Reflections |
|---|---|---|
| Take the time to state their purpose clearly. | Are often unclear about their central purpose. | Have I made the purpose of my reasoning clear? What exactly am I trying to achieve? Have I stated the purpose in several ways to clarify it? |
| Distinguish it from related purposes. | Oscillate between different, sometimes contradictory purposes. | What different purposes do I have in mind? How do I see them as related? Am I going off in somewhat different directions? How can I reconcile these contradictory purposes? |
| Periodically remind themselves of their purpose to determine whether they are straying from it. | Lose track of their fundamental object or goal. | In writing this proposal, do I seem to be wandering from my purpose? How do my third and fourth paragraph relate to my central goal? |
| Adopt realistic purposes and goals. | Adopt unrealistic purposes and set unrealistic goals. | Am I trying to accomplish too much in this project? |
| Choose significant purposes and goals. | Adopt trivial purposes and goals as if they were significant. | What is the significance of pursuing this particular purpose? Is there a more significant purpose I should be focused on? |
| Choose goals and purposes that are consistent with other goals and purposes they have chosen. | Inadvertently negate their own purposes. Do not monitor their thinking for inconsistent goals. | Does one part of my proposal seem to undermine what I am trying to accomplish in another part? |
| Adjust their thinking regularly to their purpose. | Do not adjust their thinking regularly to their purpose. | Does my argument stick to the issue? Am I acting consistently within my purpose? |
| Choose purposes that are fairminded, considering the desires and rights of others equally with their own desires and rights. | Choose purposes that are self-serving at the expense of others' needs and desires. | Is my purpose self-serving or concerned only with my own desires? Does it take into account the rights and needs of other people? |

# Questions at Issue or Central Problem

(All reasoning is an attempt to figure something out,
to settle some question, solve some problem.)

**Primary Standards:** (1) Clarity and precision, (2) Significance, (3) Answerability (4) Relevance

**Common Problems:** (1) Unclear and imprecise, (2) Insignificant, (3) Not answerable, (4) Irrelevant

**Principle:** To settle a question, it must be answerable, and you must be clear about it and understand what is needed to adequately answer it.

| Skilled Thinkers... | Unskilled Thinkers... | Critical Reflections |
|---|---|---|
| Are clear about the question they are trying to settle. | Are often unclear about the question they are asking. | Am I clear about the main question at issue? Am I able to state it precisely? |
| Can re-express a question in a variety of ways. | Express questions vaguely and find questions difficult to reformulate for clarity. | Am I able to reformulate my question in several ways to recognize the complexity of it? |
| Can break a question into sub-questions. | Are unable to break down the questions they are asking. | Have I broken down the main question into sub-questions? What are the sub-questions embedded in the main question? |
| Routinely distinguish questions of different types. | Confuse questions of different types and thus often respond inappropriately to the questions they ask. | Am I confused about the type of question I am asking? For example: Am I confusing a legal question with an ethical one? Am I confusing a question of preference with a question requiring judgment? |
| Distinguish significant from trivial questions. | Confuse trivial questions with significant ones. | Am I focusing on trivial questions while other significant questions need to be addressed? |
| Distinguish relevant questions from irrelevant ones. | Confuse irrelevant questions with relevant ones. | Are the questions I am raising in this discussion relevant to the main question at issue? |
| Are sensitive to the assumptions built into the questions they ask. | Often ask loaded questions. | Is the way I am putting the questions loaded? Am I taking for granted from the onset the correctness of my own position? |
| Distinguish questions they can answer from questions they can't. | Try to answer questions they are not in a position to answer. | Am I in a position to answer this question? What information would I need to have before I could answer the question? |

# Information

(All reasoning is based on data, information, evidence, experience, and research.)

**Primary Standards:** (1) Clear, ( 2) Relevant, (3) Fairly gathered and reported, (4) Accurate, (5) Adequate, (6) Consistently applied

**Common Problems:** (1) Unclear, (2) Irrelevant, (3) Biased, (4) Inaccurate, (5) Insufficient, (6) Inconsistently applied

**Principle:** Reasoning can be only as sound as the information upon which it is based.

| Skilled Thinkers... | Unskilled Thinkers... | Critical Reflections |
|---|---|---|
| Assert a claim only when they have sufficient evidence to back it up. | Assert claims without considering all relevant information. | Is my assertion supported by evidence? |
| Can articulate and evaluate the information behind their claims. | Do not articulate the information they are using in their reasoning and so do not subject it to rational scrutiny. | Do I have evidence to support my claim that I have not clearly articulated? Have I evaluated for accuracy and relevance the information I am using? |
| Actively search for information against (not just for) their position. | Gather information only when it supports their point of view. | Where is a good place to look for evidence on the opposite side? Have I looked there? Have I honestly considered information that does not support my position? |
| Focus on relevant information and disregard what is irrelevant to the question at issue. | Do not carefully distinguish between relevant information and irrelevant information. | Are my data relevant to the claim I am making? Have I failed to consider relevant information? |
| Draw conclusions only to the extent that they are supported by the data and sound reasoning. | Make inferences that go beyond what the data supports. | Does my claim go beyond the evidence I have cited? |
| State their evidence clearly and fairly. | Distort the data or state it inaccurately. | Is my presentation of the pertinent information clear and coherent? Have I distorted information to support my position? |

# Inference and Interpretation

(All reasoning contains inferences from which we draw conclusions and give meaning to data and situations.)

**Primary Standards:** (1) Clarity, (2) Logicality, (3) Justifiability, (4) Profundity, (5) Reasonability, (6) Consistency

**Common Problems:** (1) Unclear, (2) Illogical, (3) Unjustified, (4) Superficial, (5) Unreasonable, (6) Contradictory

**Principle:** Reasoning can be only as sound as the inferences it makes (or the conclusions to which it comes).

| Skilled Thinkers... | Unskilled Thinkers... | Critical Reflections |
|---|---|---|
| Are clear about the inferences they are making.<br>Clearly articulate their inferences. | Are often unclear about the inferences they are making.<br>Do not clearly articulate their inferences. | Am I clear about the inferences I am making?<br>Have I clearly articulated my conclusions? |
| Usually make inferences that follow from the evidence or reasons presented. | Often make inferences that do not follow from the evidence or reasons presented. | Do my conclusions logically follow from the evidence and reasons presented? |
| Often make inferences that are deep rather than superficial. | Often make inferences that are superficial. | Are my conclusions superficial, given the problem? |
| Often make inferences or come to conclusions that are reasonable. | Often make inferences or come to conclusions that are unreasonable. | Are my conclusions unreasonable? |
| Make inferences or come to conclusions that are consistent with each other. | Often make inferences or come to conclusions that are contradictory. | Do the conclusions I reach in the first part of my analysis seem to contradict the conclusions that I come to at the end? |
| Understand the assumptions that lead to inferences. | Do not seek to figure out the assumptions that lead to inferences. | Is my inference based on a faulty assumption?<br>How would my inference be changed if I were to base it on a different, more justifiable assumption? |

# Assumptions

(All reasoning is based on assumptions—beliefs we take for granted.)

**Primary Standards:** (1) Clarity, (2) Justifiability, (3) Consistency
**Common Problems:** (1) Unclear, (2) Unjustified, (3) Contradictory
**Principle:** Reasoning can be only as sound as the assumptions on which it is based.

| Skilled Thinkers... | Unskilled Thinkers... | Critical Reflections |
|---|---|---|
| Are clear about the assumptions they are making. | Are often unclear about the assumptions they make. | Are my assumptions clear to me?<br>Do I clearly understand what my assumptions are based on? |
| Make assumptions that are reasonable and justifiable given the situation and evidence. | Often make unjustified or unreasonable assumptions. | Do I make assumptions about the future based on just one experience from the past?<br>Can I fully justify what I am taking for granted?<br>Are my assumptions justifiable given the evidence I am using to support them? |
| Make assumptions that are consistent with each other. | Make assumptions that are contradictory. | Do the assumptions I made in the first part of my argument contradict the assumptions I am making now? |
| Constantly seek to discern and understand their assumptions. | Ignore their assumptions. | What assumptions am I making in this situation?<br>Are they justifiable?<br>Where did I get these assumptions? |

# Concepts and Ideas

(All reasoning is expressed through, and shaped by, concepts and ideas.)

**Primary Standards:** (1) Clarity, (2) Relevancy, (3) Depth, (4) Accuracy
**Common Problems:** (1) Unclear, (2) Irrelevant, (3) Superficial, (4) Inaccurate
**Principle:** Reasoning can be only as sound as the assumptions on which it is based.

| Skilled Thinkers... | Unskilled Thinkers... | Critical Reflections |
|---|---|---|
| Recognize the key concepts and ideas they and others use. | Are unaware of the key concepts and ideas they and others use. | What is the main concept I am using in my thinking? What are the main concepts others are using? |
| Are able to explain the basic implications of the key words and phrases they use. | Cannot accurately explain basic implications of their key words and phrases. | Am I clear about the implications of key concepts? For example: Does the word "argument" have negative implications that the word "rationale" does not? |
| Distinguish special, nonstandard uses of words from standard uses, and avoid jargon in inappropriate settings. | Do not recognize when their use of a word or phrase or symbol departs from conventional or disciplinary usage. | Where did I get my definitions of this central concept? Is it consistent with convention? Have I put unwarranted conclusions into the definition? Does any of my vocabulary have special connotations that others may not recognize? Have I been careful to define any specialized terms, abbreviations, or mathematical symbols? Have I avoided jargon where possible? |
| Recognize irrelevant concepts and ideas and use concepts and ideas in ways relevant to their functions. | Use concepts or theories in ways inappropriate to the subject or issue. | Am I using the concept of "efficiency" appropriately? For example: Have I confused "efficiency" and "effectiveness"? Am I applying theories which do not apply to this application? |
| Think deeply about the concepts they use. | Fail to think deeply about the concepts they use. | Am I thinking deeply enough about this concept? For example: The concept of product safety or durability, as I describe it, does not take into account inexpert customers. Do I need to consider the idea of product safety more deeply? |

# Point of View

(All reasoning is done from some point of view.)

**Primary Standards:** (1) Flexibility, (2) Fairness, (3) Clarity, (4) Breadth, (5) Relevance

**Common Problems:** (1) Restricted, (2) Biased, (3) Unclear, (4) Narrow, (5) Irrelevant

**Principle:** To reason well, you must identify those points of view relevant to the issue and enter these viewpoints empathetically.

| Skilled Thinkers... | Unskilled Thinkers... | Critical Reflections |
|---|---|---|
| Keep in mind that people have different points of view, especially on controversial issues. | Dismiss or disregard alternative reasonable viewpoints. | Have I articulated the point of view from which I am approaching this issue? Have I considered opposing points of view regarding this issue? |
| Consistently articulate other points of view and reason from within those points of view to adequately understand other points of view. | Cannot see issues from points of view that are significantly different from their own. Cannot reason with empathy from alien points of view. | I may have characterized my own point of view, but have I considered the most significant aspects of the problem from the point of view of others? |
| Seek other viewpoints, especially when the issue is one they believe in passionately. | Recognize other points of view when the issue is not emotionally charged, but cannot do so for issues about which they feel strongly. | Am I expressing X's point of view in an unfair manner? Am I having difficulty appreciating X's viewpoint because I am emotional about this issue? |
| Confine their monological reasoning to problems that are clearly monological.* | Confuse multilogical with monological issues; insists that there is only one frame of reference within which a given multilogical question must be decided. | Is the question here monological or multilogical? How can I tell? Am I reasoning as if only one point of view is relevant to this issue when in reality other viewpoints are relevant? |
| Recognize when they are most likely to be prejudiced. | Are unaware of their own prejudices. | Is this prejudiced or reasoned judgment? If prejudiced, where does it originate? |
| Approach problems and issues with a richness of vision and an appropriately broad point of view. | Reason from within inappropriately narrow or superficial points of view. | Is my approach to this question too narrow? Am I considering other viewpoints so I can adequately address the problem? |

\* Monological problems are ones for which there are definite correct and incorrect answers and definite procedures for getting those answers. In multilogical problems, there are competing schools of thought to be considered.

# Implications and Consequences

(All reasoning leads somewhere. It has implications and,
when acted upon, has consequences.)

**Primary Standards:** (1) Significance, (2) Logicality, (3) Clarity, (4) Precision, (5) Completeness

**Common Problems:** (1) Unimportant, (2) Unrealistic, (3) Unclear, (4) Imprecise, (5) Incomplete

**Principle:** To reason well through an issue, you might think through the implications that follow from your reasoning. You must think through the consequences likely to flow from the decisions you make.

| Skilled Thinkers... | Unskilled Thinkers... | Critical Reflections |
|---|---|---|
| Trace out a number of significant potential implications and consequences of their reasoning. | Trace out few or none of the implications and consequences of holding a position or making a decision. | Did I spell out all the significant consequences of the action I am advocating? If I were to take this course of action, what other consequences might follow that I have not considered? Have I considered all plausible failures? |
| Clearly and precisely articulate the possible implications and consequences. | Are unclear and imprecise in the possible consequences they articulate. | Have I delineated clearly and precisely the consequences likely to follow from my chosen actions? |
| Search for potentially negative as well as potentially positive consequences. | Trace out only the consequence they had in mind at the beginning, either positive or negative, but usually not both. | I may have done a good job of spelling out some positive implications of the decision I am about to make, but what are some of the possible negative implications or consequences. |
| Anticipate the likelihood of unexpected negative and positive implications. | Are surprised when their decisions have unexpected consequences. | If I make this decision, what are some possible unexpected implications? What are some of the variables out of my control that might lead to negative consequences? |
| Considers the reactions of all parties. | Assumes the outcomes and products will be welcomed by other parties. | What measures are appropriate to inform the community or marketplace? What opinion leaders should be involved? |

# The Questioning Mind in Engineering:
# The Wright Brothers[6]

Throughout history, there have been a plethora of engineers who were not only clear thinkers but stunning visionaries as well. In the preindustrial age, many who were important scientists were also engineers (Da Vinci, Galileo, Franklin, Fulton). Indeed, the ancient artifacts of many brilliant engineers grace the landscapes of China, Egypt, and Rome's Empire. For our brief purpose, two exemplars will suffice to illustrate highly skilled engineering reasoning. Orville and Wilbur Wright rank among history's most influential personalities, having profoundly contributed to our modern lifestyles.

We all recognize the photo of Orville's first flight, the Flyer hanging in air, the expectant Wilbur poised, watching. This 1903 snapshot represents a six-year campaign from the 1899 spark of the Wright brothers' interest in aeronautics to their first practical airplane in 1905.

Throughout that campaign, the brothers proved themselves master thinkers, propelled by good questions. The record of their letters and papers shows resolute and unflinching purpose. They clearly articulated the dominant questions to be resolved, and practiced what we now call "Systems Engineering" by articulating the need to integrate their solutions to the particular problems of propulsion, structures, aerodynamics, and control. They actively corresponded with others, mining the best of the common pool of existing knowledge. Yet, where necessary, they questioned the validity of others' data and created experiments to correct identified errors and gaps. They recognized the impact of their assumptions, carefully accounting for the limitations of their small-scale testing in wind tunnels or across the handles of a moving bicycle. They questioned conventional concepts; they were first to describe propellers as a twisted, rotating wing, supplanting the flawed conception of a propeller as analogous to a machine screw.

---

6 Sources: Jakab P. *Visions of a Flying Machine*; McFarland MW (ed.). *The Papers of Wilbur and Orville Wright*; and Anderson J. *The History of Aerodynamics*. Photograph: public domain.

The Wrights had broad foresight, realizing that they needed to be both inventors and pilots. They devoted 1,000 glider flights to learning to fly prior to the first powered flight. Their progress represented numerous intermediate conclusions and inferences drawn from their progressive learning—each year's variant drawing heavily on the lessons learned from the prior year's flying and experiments. They were cognizant of implications, giving particular attention to managing the hazards associated with flight tests, ensuring that they would survive the inevitable crashes.

They distinguished themselves from others pursuing the same goal by the breadth and depth of the questions they posed and pursued. They did not see their challenge as a narrow aerodynamic or technical one, but broadly, as a complex challenge involving multiple technologies. The comical footage we see of others' halting attempts at powered flight reveals ignorance of its complexities. Competitors ignored stability, or drag, or weight, or embraced shallow and erroneous concepts of flight. Others' designs seem to cry, "Surely if it flaps like a bird, it will fly like a bird." In contrast, the Wrights' papers indicate a methodical integrated series of questions and answers posed from diverse points of view as inventors, scientists, businessmen, and pilots. Herein lay their success.

# The Cost of Thinking Gone Awry

On February 1, 2003, the space shuttle Columbia disintegrated over the southern U.S., killing its crew of seven. The Columbia Accident Investigation Board (CAIB) met over the months that followed to identify the direct and indirect causes, and provide both NASA and the U.S. Congress with concrete direction with respect to the future of both the shuttle program and American manned space flight.[7] The direct technical causes of this tragedy have been widely publicized. More significantly, the CAIB reserved its most scathing findings for an institutional culture within NASA fraught with poor thinking practices that appeared to have learned nothing from the 1986 loss of the space shuttle Challenger.

Note the use of our critical thinking vocabulary in the following causal factors identified by the CAIB report, and rife throughout NASA and its contractors.

- Failure to challenge *assumptions* or patterns
- Unsupported/illogical *inferences*
- *Assumptions* confused with *inferences*
- Suppression/dismissal of *dissenting views*
- Failure to *evaluate data* quality or recognize data deficits
- Failure to weigh the full range of *implications*
- Narrow *points of view*
- Confused *purposes*
- Failure to pose the appropriate *questions*
- Application of irrelevant data and *concepts*
- Vague, equivocal language

The CAIB report specifically charged NASA leadership with a reformation of their culture to improve and encourage good thinking across the agency and its supporting contractors. The promotion of good thinking practices was to be designed into the organizational structure.

---

7 Gehman, HW, et. al. 2003. *Columbia Accident Investigation Board Report*, vol. 1. http://caib.nasa.gov/news/report/volume1/default.html.

# Noteworthy Connections and Distinctions

People often view science and engineering as almost synonymous, likely due to the criticality of science to most engineering work and the content of an engineering education. We have already noted a number of distinctions and similarities between the kinds of questions posed by the scientist and engineer. The topics in this section give rise to additional interesting questions at the junction of the engineer's role and that of others with whom engineers might work.

## Creativity in Engineering

Engineering is a creative enterprise. Even the simplest engineering jobs require analysis and assessment, yet will also demand ingenuity and creativity in applying concepts, tools, and materials to the problem at hand. Problems with unique solutions are rare, requiring judgment to discern the strengths and weaknesses of candidate solutions. Design requirements are frequently in tension, necessitating creativity and keen insight into the customer's application to appropriately balance those tensions. True technical innovation permits the creation of systems or products with novel capabilities.

- Do the technical requirements require a new approach or technology?
- What is the market for, cost of, or schedule risk of innovation on this project?
- What opportunity does innovation create in this project?

## Engineering and Aesthetics

It's not all about the numbers. Unattractive products usually don't sell. Consequently, the skilled engineer cannot ignore the aesthetic implications of their finished work. Indeed, in many engineering enterprises, engineering teams will either include or consult professional designers to ensure a product's aesthetic appeal. History is replete with engineers who were keenly aware of the importance of aesthetics, leaving us with bridges, buildings, steam locomotives, ships, and so on, in which form and function harmoniously and attractively served one another.

- To what extent should I be concerned with the design's aesthetic appeal? Does the marketing department agree? Does the customer agree?
- Is professional design consultation appropriate to this project?

## Engineering and Technicians

While both engineers and technicians are technologists, in the sense that their work is technologically based, there are significant differences in how the two words are commonly used. "Technician" typically applies to those skilled trades involved with the manufacture, maintenance, or repair of technical systems. An engineering degree is seldom required of a technician (nor math beyond algebra and trigonometry). However, considerable post-secondary training may be required for technicians in many fields. In many situations, it is common to find technicians and engineers working together within teams. Technicians might commonly ask, "How do I restore the equipment to its optimum operating condition?" The in-service engineer working with him might instead ask, "How can the equipment be redesigned to avoid this failure in the future or facilitate future repair?"

## Engineers and Craftsmen

Overlap exists between the role of the engineer and a craftsman. "Craftsman" typically connotes technical skill blended with artistry, and might well express technical work in innovative ways. The craftsman might consider many of the factors about which engineers are concerned. For example, a cabinetry maker might carefully select the materials for a particular application on the basis of strength and durability, selecting joints and fasteners based upon the anticipated load. The engineer would typically approach a similar task by way of numerical analysis, whereas a craftsman might generally approach the task intuitively, based on experience with both the materials and usage. Many engineers have little direct fabrication experience, while craftsmanship typically connotes direct fabrication of a product. Orville and Wilbur Wright provide an interesting example. As inventors of the airplane, carefully calculating the required elements of each part of the design, they were "thinking" as engineers. As bicycle makers, primarily relying upon intuition and past experience, they appear to have been "thinking" as craftsmen.

## Engineering and Public Policy

Public policy frequently influences the practice of engineering. This can result from the regulation of some perceived public or consumer hazard, or the export control of a defense-sensitive technology. In these cases, policy may constrain or oppose good engineering practice. In others, public policy may foster engineering activity or innovation in the form of contracts, research grants, or tax credits. The engineer working in the public domain must have intellectual empathy, must be able to grasp the concerns and interests expressed by agents of public entities (regulators, lawmakers, contracting officers), who may not have technical education or experience. It is commonplace for policy requirements or specifications designed to reduce or eliminate hazards to instead hinder or constrain developing technologies or the work of the engineer. It is therefore frequently appropriate for the engineer to probe with questions of relevance when technology has moved faster than the public policy, or when public interest is not served by overzealous policy (e.g., consider the often excessively large number of rules and regulations in building).

# Ethics and Engineering

The work of engineering has implications for helping or harming living creatures, and for improving or diminishing the quality of life on earth. Therefore, the highly skilled engineer is concerned with the ethical implications of engineering discoveries and inventions, and the potential of engineering for both good and ill.

The ethical responsibilities of engineers are similar to that of scientists, because the implications of engineering are often similar to implications of science. It is useful to consider the transformation that Einstein underwent in his views regarding the ethical responsibilities of scientist. "From regarding scientists as a group almost aloof from the rest of the world, he began to consider them first as having responsibilities and rights level with the rest of men, and finally as a group whose exceptional position demanded the exercise of exceptional responsibilities." In 1948, after the United States dropped atomic bombs on Hiroshima and Nagasaki, Einstein wrote this message to the World Congress of Intellectuals.

> We scientists, whose tragic destiny it has been to help make the methods of annihilation ever more gruesome and more effective, must consider it our solemn and transcendent duty to do all in our power in preventing these weapons from being used for the brutal purpose for which they were invented. What task could possibly be more important to us? What social aim could be closer to our hearts?[8]

It is critical that engineers keep the ethical implications of their work near the forefront of their decisions. This includes thinking through ethical implications of normal operations, possible failure modes, and even situations in which a product might be misused by the customer (e.g., situations, conditions, or applications not intended by the designer). The capacity for harm motivates governmental regulation and licensure of engineers in many fields. However, while many engineering responsibilities may be codified in applicable law, ethical duty exists even where legal obligation does not.[9]

## Humanitarian Responsibility and Product Safety

All engineers bear an obvious ethical responsibility to avoid compromising the health and welfare of those who purchase their products, as well as those who might come into contact with their product, whether it is a consumer product or a suspension bridge. Moreover, while all engineers presumably make products with beneficial purposes, some engineers have positive ethical opportunities to dramatically contribute to the health, welfare, and economic vitality of individuals and communities.

*Collapse of the Tacoma*

---

[8]  Clark R.1984. Einstein: The Life and Times. New York: Avon Books, 723.

[9]  National Society of Professional Engineers. 2003. *Code of Ethics for Engineers*. www.nspe.org/ethics/codeofethics2003.pdf

## Fiduciary Responsibility

Engineers have fiduciary responsibilities to customers, company leadership, and stockholders. However, neither customers nor stockholders have detailed insight into the engineer's daily activity or design decisions. Consequently, it is the engineer's duty to safeguard the interests and points of view of these stakeholders, as a matter of ethical responsibility.

## Environmental Responsibility

Large-scale catastrophes such as Bhopal or Chernobyl draw the principal attention as exemplars of the power of engineers for destructive impacts on communities, regions, and nations. In these cases, a single product failure broadly devastated lives, livelihoods, and property. As substantial, however, are the recurring cumulative effects of normally functioning products whose count may number in the tens of thousands, but whose pollutant products, consumption of resources, or disposal challenges impose detrimental environmental and/or economic effects over time.

In short, where there are ethical implications of an engineer's work for the health and sustainability of the earth, the engineer has inescapable ethical obligations.

# Engineering Reasoning Objectives

The CDIO (Conceive–Design–Implement–Operate) consortium has developed a comprehensive syllabus for an engineering education, ratified by diverse international industry and academic leaders.[10] The syllabus articulates a diverse range of learning objectives, many of which explicitly employ the language of critical thinking. This list is of principle benefit to educators seeking to catalog program educational outcomes.

## Engineering Affective Dimensions
- Exercising independent thought and judgment (2.4.2)[11]
- Exercising reciprocity (2.4.2)
- Welcoming ingenuity and innovation (2.4.1, 2.4.3)
- Recognizing diverse stakeholder points of view (2.3.1, 4.1.6)
- Suspending judgment (2.4.2)
- Developing insight into egocentrism and sociocentrism (2.4.2)

## Cognitive Dimensions: Engineering Macro-Abilities
- Selecting critical questions to be answered (2.2.1)
- Clarifying technical issues and claims (2.2.1)
- Clarifying technological ideas (2.1, 2.2, 3.2)
- Developing criteria for technical evaluation (4.4.6)
- Evaluating scientific/engineering authorities (2.2.2)
- Raising and pursuing root questions (2.2.1)
- Evaluating technical arguments (2.4.4)
- Generating and assessing solutions to engineering problems (2.1)
- Identifying and clarifying relevant points of view (4.2)
- Engaging in Socratic discussion and dialectical thinking on engineering issues
- Avoiding oversimplification of issues
- Developing engineering perspective (4.x)

## Cognitive Dimensions: Engineering Micro-Skills
- Evaluating data (2.1.1)
- Analyzing assumptions (2.1.1)
- Identifying and applying appropriate models (2.1.2)
- Explaining generalizations (2.1.3)
- Questioning incomplete or ambiguous information (2.1.4)
- Analyzing essential results of solutions and test data (2.1.5)
- Reconciling discrepancies in results (2.1.5)
- Making plausible engineering inferences (2.1)
- Supplying appropriate evidence for a design conclusion (4.4)
- Recognizing contradictions
- Recognizing technical, legal/regulatory, economic, environmental, and safety implications and consequences (4.1.1)
- Distinguishing facts from engineering principles, values, and ideas

---

[10] See www.cdio.org for more details.

[11] Codes refer to syllabus topics in the CDIO syllabus.

# Evaluating Student Work in Engineering

## The Grade of F

F-level work fails to display an understanding of the basic nature of engineering reasoning, and in any case does not display the engineering skills and abilities, which are at the heart of this course. The work at the end of the course is as vague, imprecise, and unreasoned as it was in the beginning. There is little evidence that the student is genuinely engaged in the task of taking charge of his or her engineering reasoning. Many assignments appear to have been done pro forma, the student simply going through the motions without really putting any significant effort into thinking his or her way through them. Consequently, the student is not analyzing engineering problems clearly, not formulating information accurately, not distinguishing relevant from irrelevant information, not identifying key questionable assumptions, not clarifying key concepts, not reasoning carefully from clearly stated premises, or tracing implications and consequences. The student's work does not display discernable engineering reasoning and problem-solving skills.

## The Grade of D

D-level work shows only a minimal level understanding of what engineering is, along with the development of some, but very little, engineering skills or abilities. D-level work at the end of the course shows occasional engineering reasoning, but frequent uncritical thinking. Most assignments are poorly done. There is little evidence that the student is "reasoning" through the assignment. Often the student seems to be merely going through the motions of the assignment, carrying out the form without getting into the spirit of it. D-level work rarely shows any effort to take charge of ideas, assumptions, inferences, and intellectual processes. In general, D-level thinking lacks discipline and clarity. In D-level work, the student rarely analyzes engineering problems clearly and precisely, almost never formulates information accurately, rarely distinguishes the relevant from the irrelevant, rarely recognizes key assumptions, almost never describes key concepts effectively, frequently fails to use engineering vocabulary in keeping with established professional usage, and seldom reasons carefully from clearly stated premises, or recognizes important implications and consequences. D-level work frequently displays poor engineering reasoning and problem-solving skills.

## The Grade of C

C-level work illustrates inconsistent achievement in grasping what engineering is, along with the development of modest engineering skills or abilities. C-level work at the end of the course shows some emerging engineering skills, but also pronounced weaknesses as well. Though some assignments are reasonably well done, others are poorly done; or at best are mediocre. There are more than occasional lapses in reasoning. Though engineering terms and distinctions are sometimes used effectively, sometimes they are used quite ineffectively. Only on occasion does C-level work display a mind taking charge of its own ideas, assumptions, inferences, and intellectual processes. Only occasionally does C-level work display intellectual discipline and clarity. The C-level student only occasionally analyzes problems clearly and precisely, formulates information accurately, distinguishes the relevant from the irrelevant, recognizes key questionable assumptions, clarifies key concepts effectively, uses vocabulary in keeping with established professional usage, and reasons carefully from clearly stated premises, or recognizes important engineering implications and consequences. Sometimes the C-level student seems to be simply going through the motions of the assignment, carrying out the form without getting into the spirit of it. On the whole, C-level work shows only modest and inconsistent engineering reasoning and problem-solving skills.

## The Grade of B

B-level work represents demonstrable achievement in grasping what engineering is, along with the clear demonstration of a range of specific engineering skills or abilities. B-level work at the end of the course is, on the whole, clear, precise, and well-reasoned, though with occasional lapses into weak reasoning. Overall, engineering terms and distinctions are used effectively. The work demonstrates a mind beginning to take charge of its own ideas, assumptions, inferences, and intellectual processes. The student often analyzes engineering problems clearly and precisely, often formulates information accurately, usually distinguishes the relevant from the irrelevant, and often recognizes key questionable assumptions, usually clarifies key concepts effectively. The student typically uses engineering language in keeping with established professional usage, and shows a general tendency to reason carefully from clearly stated premises, as well as noticeable sensitivity to important implications and consequences. B-level work displays good engineering reasoning and problem-solving skills.

## The Grade of A

A-level work demonstrates advanced achievement in grasping what engineering is, along with the comprehensive development of a range of specific engineering skills or abilities. The work at the end of the course is, on the whole, clear, precise, and well-reasoned, though with occasional lapses into weak reasoning. In A-level work, engineering terms and distinctions are used effectively. The work demonstrates a mind beginning to take charge of its own ideas, assumptions, inferences, and intellectual processes. The A-level student often analyzes engineering problems clearly and precisely, often formulates information accurately, usually distinguishes the relevant from the irrelevant, often recognizes key questionable assumptions, and usually clarifies key concepts effectively. The student typically uses engineering language in keeping with established professional usage, frequently identifies relevant competing points of view, and shows a general tendency to reason carefully from clearly stated premises, as well as noticeable sensitivity to important implications and consequences. A-level work displays excellent engineering reasoning and problem-solving skills. The A student's work is consistently at a high level of intellectual excellence.

# The Problem of Egocentric Thinking

Egocentric thinking results from the unfortunate fact that humans do not naturally consider the rights and needs of others. They do not naturally appreciate the point of view of others nor the limitations in their own point of view. They become explicitly aware of their egocentric thinking only if trained to do so. They do not naturally recognize their egocentric assumptions, the egocentric way they use information, the egocentric way they interpret data, the source of their egocentric concepts and ideas, the implications of their egocentric thought. They do not naturally recognize their self-serving perspective.

As humans they live with the unrealistic but confident sense that they have fundamentally figured out the way things actually are, and that they have done this objectively. They naturally believe in their intuitive perceptions—however inaccurate. Instead of using intellectual standards in thinking, they often use self-centered psychological standards to determine what to believe and what to reject. Here are the most commonly used psychological standards in human thinking.

"IT'S TRUE BECAUSE I BELIEVE IT." Innate egocentrism: I assume that what I believe is true even though I have never questioned the basis for many of my beliefs.

"IT'S TRUE BECAUSE WE BELIEVE IT." Innate sociocentrism: I assume that the dominant beliefs within the groups to which I belong are true even though I have never questioned the basis for many of these beliefs.

"IT'S TRUE BECAUSE I WANT TO BELIEVE IT." Innate wish fulfillment: I believe in, for example, accounts of behavior that put me (or the groups to which I belong) in a positive rather than a negative light even though I have not seriously considered the evidence for the more negative account. I believe what "feels good," what supports my other beliefs, what does not require me to change my thinking in any significant way, what does not require me to admit I have been wrong.

"IT'S TRUE BECAUSE I HAVE ALWAYS BELIEVED IT." Innate self-validation: I have a strong desire to maintain beliefs that I have long held, even though I have not seriously considered the extent to which those beliefs are justified, given the evidence.

"IT'S TRUE BECAUSE IT IS IN MY SELFISH INTEREST TO BELIEVE IT" Innate selfishness: I hold fast to beliefs that justify my getting more power, money, or personal advantage even though these beliefs are not grounded in sound reasoning or evidence.

Because humans are naturally prone to assess thinking in keeping with the above criteria, it is not surprising that we, as a species, have not developed a significant interest in establishing and teaching legitimate intellectual standards. It is not surprising that our thinking is often flawed. We are truly the "self-deceived animal."

# Stages of Critical Thinking Development[12]

**Accomplished Thinker**
(Intellectual skills
and virtues have
become second
nature in our lives)

**Advanced Thinker**
(We are committed to
lifelong practice and are
beginning to internalize
intellectual virtues)

**Practicing Thinker**
(We regularly practice and
advance accordingly)

**Beginning Thinker**
(We try to improve but without regular practice)

**Challenged Thinker**
(We are faced with significant
problems in our thinking)

**Unreflective Thinker**
(We are unaware of significant
problems in our thinking)

---

[12] Found in *Critical Thinking: Tools for Take Charge of Your Professional and Personal Life*, second edition, by Richard Paul and Linda Elder (2014). Upper Saddle River: Pearson Education..

# The Thinker's Guide Library

Rowman & Littlefield is the proud distributor of the Thinker's Guide Library developed by the Foundation for Critical Thinking. Please visit www.rowman.com or call 1-800-462-640 for more information. Bulk order discounts available.

 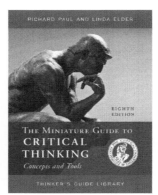 

## For Everyone

**The Miniature Guide to Critical Thinking Concepts & Tools, Eighth Edition**
Paperback 9781538134948
eBook 9781538134955

**The Thinker's Guide to Ethical Reasoning**
Paperback 9780944583173
eBook 9781538133781

**The Thinker's Guide to Fallacies**
Paperback 9780944583272
eBook 9781538133774

**The Art of Asking Essential Questions**
Paperback 9780944583166
eBook 9781538133804

**The Thinker's Guide for Conscientious Citizens on How to Detect Media Bias and Propaganda in National and World News, Fourth Edition**
Paperback 9780944583203
eBook 9781538133897

**The Thinker's Guide to Engineering Reasoning**
Paperback 9780944583333
eBook 9781538133798

**The Thinker's Guide to Analytic Thinking**
Paperback 9780944583197
eBook 9781538133750

**The Thinker's Guide to Socratic Questioning**
Paperback 9780944583319
eBook 9781538133842

**The Nature and Functions of Critical & Creative Thinking**
Paperback 9780944583265
eBook 9781538133958

**Thinker's Guide to the Human Mind**
Paperback 9780944583586
eBook 9781538133880

**The Thinker's Guide to Scientific Thinking**
Paperback 9780985754426
eBook 9781538133811

**The Thinker's Guide to Clinical Reasoning**
Paperback 9780944583425
eBook 9781538133873

## For Students

**The Aspiring Thinker's Guide to Critical Thinking**
Paperback 9780944583418
eBook 9781538133767

**The Thinker's Guide for Students on How to Study & Learn a Discipline, Second Edition**
Paperback 9781632340009
eBook 9781538133835

**The International Critical Thinking Reading and Writing Test, Second Edition**
Paperback 9780944583326
eBook 9781538133965

**The Student Guide to Historical Thinking**
Paperback 9780944583463
eBook 9781538133941

**How to Read a Paragraph, second edition**
Paperback 9780944583494
eBook 9781538133828

**How to Write a Paragraph**
Paperback 9780944583227
eBook 9781538133866

## For Educators

**The Miniature Guide to Practical Ways for Promoting Active and Cooperative Learning, Third Edition**
Paperback 9780944583135
eBook 9781538133903

**A Critical Thinker's Guide to Educational Fads**
Paperback 9780944583340
eBook 9781538133910

**A Guide for Educators to Critical Thinking Competency Standards**
Paperback 9780944583302
eBook 9781538133934

**How to Improve Student Learning: 30 Practical Ideas**
Paperback 9780944583555
eBook 9781538133859

**The Thinker's Guide to Intellectual Standards**
Paperback 9780944583395
eBook 9781538133927